Backyard Birds of the East

Krista Einstein
Genevieve Einstein

KidsWorld

Quick Guide

These are some of the birds that you are most likely to see in your backyard if you live in Eastern North America. We've included their measurements in case you want to have fun with rulers!

Cooper's Hawk p. 8

Length: 15 in (38 cm)

American Kestrel p. 10

Length: 10 in (25 cm)

Ring-billed Gull p. 12

Length: 19 in (49 cm)

Rock Pigeon p. 14

Length: 13 in (33 cm)

Mourning Dove p. 16

Length: 11 in (29 cm)

Barred Owl p. 18

Length: 19 in (48 cm)

Ruby-throated Hummingbird p. 20

Length: 3 in (8 cm)

Downy Woodpecker p. 22

Length: 6 in (16 cm)

Northern Flicker p. 24

Length: 12 in (30 cm)

**Pileated
Woodpecker p. 26**
Length: 18 in (45 cm)

**Great Crested
Flycatcher p. 28**
Length: 8 in (20 cm)

Red-eyed Vireo p. 30
Length: 5 in (13 cm)

Blue Jay p. 32
Length: 11 in (28 cm)

**American
Crow p. 34**
Length: 18 in (47 cm)

Barn Swallow p. 36
Length: 7 in (18 cm)

**Black-capped
Chickadee p. 38**
Length: 5 in (13 cm)

Tufted Titmouse p. 40
Length: 6 in (15 cm)

**Red-breasted
Nuthatch p. 42**
Length: 4 in (10 cm)

**White-breasted
Nuthatch p. 44**
Length: 5 in (13 cm)

House Wren p. 46
Length: 5 in (13 cm)

**Golden-crowned
Kinglet p. 48**
Length: 4 in (10 cm)

**Eastern
Bluebird p. 50**
Length: 7 in (18 cm)

**American
Robin p. 52**
Length: 10 in (25 cm)

Gray Catbird p. 54
Length: 9 in (23 cm)

**European
Starling p. 56**
Length: 9 in (23 cm)

Cedar Waxwing p. 58
Length: 6 in (16 cm)

**Yellow-rumped
Warbler p. 60**
Length: 5 in (13 cm)

**Common
Yellowthroat p. 62**
Length: 5 in (13 cm)

**Eastern
Towhee p. 64**
Length: 8 in (20 cm)

**Chipping
Sparrow p. 66**
Length: 5 in (13 cm)

Song Sparrow p. 68
Length: 6 in (14 cm)

**White-throated
Sparrow p. 70**
Length: 6 in (16 cm)

**Dark-eyed
Junco p. 72**
Length: 6 in (16 cm)

**Scarlet
Tanager p. 74**
Length: 6 in (16 cm)

**Northern
Cardinal p. 76**
Length: 9 in (23 cm)

**Rose-breasted
Grosbeak p. 78**
Length: 7 in (18 cm)

**Red-winged
Blackbird p. 80**
Length: 8 in (20 cm)

**Common
Grackle p. 82**
Length: 13 in (32 cm)

**Brown-headed
Cowbird p. 84**
Length: 8 in (20 cm)

**Baltimore
Oriole p. 86**
Length: 7 in (18 cm)

House Finch p. 88
Length: 6 in (15 cm)

**Common
Redpoll p. 90**
Length: 5 in (13 cm)

**American
Goldfinch p. 92**
Length: 5 in (13 cm)

House Sparrow p. 94
Length: 6 in (16 cm)

How to Use this Book

Each bird in this book has icons in the top right-hand corner. These icons quickly tell you the size of the bird, where to look for it, the food it eats and the kind of nest it builds.

Size

Tiny is for birds that are shorter than the length of a pen (5 in/13 cm).

Small is for birds that are longer than the length of a pen but shorter than the length of a school ruler (6 in–1 ft/15–30 cm).

Medium is for birds that are between one and two school rulers long (1–2 ft/30–60 cm).

Large is for birds that are bigger than two school rulers placed end to end (2 ft/60 cm).

Where to Look

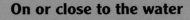
On or close to the ground

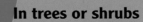
On or close to the water

In trees or shrubs

In the air

Food

 Seeds, flowers or other plant parts

 Fruits or berries

 Insects or other creepy crawlies

 Fish or other water animals

 Land animals (like mice) or birds

Nests

Simple nests are often on the ground. Birds don't put much effort into simple nests.

Cup-shaped nests are usually found in trees. These are often made with grass and twigs.

Some birds like to nest in tree cavities or nest boxes.

Some birds have nests that are unusual. They don't fit into the other categories.

Cooper's Hawk

The Cooper's Hawk regularly visits backyards to find its lunch. It is interested in bird feeders, not for the seeds, but for the birds the seeds attract. It also eats squirrels and rabbits.

Q: What do you call a hawk crossed with a lawn mower? A: A mow-hawk!

The Cooper's Hawk likes backyard birdbaths. After having a bath, it will usually move to a sunny perch to dry its feathers.

Young Cooper's Hawks are brown and white. All Cooper's Hawks have long tails and strong, sharp talons.

American Kestrel

The American Kestrel is the smallest falcon in North America. The male has a rust-colored back and blue wings. The female is rust-colored overall. Both have black barring, as well as a black moustache and sideburns.

Kestrels are common birds, often seen perching on telephone wires near grassy fields. They may come to your yard to catch mice or insects, like grasshoppers and dragonflies.

The American Kestrel makes its nest in abandoned woodpecker cavities or nest boxes. The female lays 4 to 5 eggs. Both parents take turns incubating the eggs and feeding nestlings.

11

Ring-billed Gull

In the winter, the Ring-billed Gull is seen in hanging out in parking lots or city parks. At this time of year, its head has gray spots on it.

Ring-billed Gulls aren't picky about what they eat. They will steal all kinds of food, like fruit, peanuts and even French fries, if you aren't watching!

Speckled nestlings look very different from adults.

In their first winter, young birds already have the black ring on the tip of their bill. They have more brown in their feathers than adults.

13

Rock Pigeon

Rock Pigeons **are common in backyards and parks. Most birds are gray with shiny feathers on their necks, but Rock Pigeons can also be brown or white.**

Rock Pigeons strut around on the ground, making cooing sounds. When attracting a mate, the male will fan his tail and bow his head. He may even feed her crop milk from a pouch in his throat!

Baby pigeons are called squabs. When their feathers first start to grow in, they look a bit more like porcupine quills than feathers!

15

Mourning Dove

The Mourning Dove eats seeds from the ground or from platform feeders. It also swallows small stones or grit to help it break down the tough seeds.

The Mourning Dove's wings whistle when it flies, especially during takeoff. A group of doves is called a flight of doves.

The Mourning Dove makes its nest in a tree or on the ground. It lays 2 eggs in a nest but can build a few nests each year.

Both parents look after the young. Mourning Doves feed their nestlings crop milk, which they make from the seeds they eat. It is stored in a pouch in the throat called a crop.

Barred Owl

The Barred Owl has a haunting call that sounds like who cooks for you, who cooks for you? Owls are more vocal at dawn and dusk, when the sky is clear and the moon is full.

These birds prefer to live near water, in swampy woods or forested ravines. But Barred Owls can also adapt to new habitats. More and more, they are found in forested city parks.

These owls have dark eyes, horizontal bars on their breast and vertical streaks on their belly.

Owls have good night vision and excellent hearing. They have circles of feathers around their eyes called facial discs. These discs funnel sound toward the owl's ears to help them locate prey. They listen for movement, like a mouse running through the leaves.

Ruby-throated Hummingbird

The Ruby-throated Hummingbird can fly in any direction and beat its wings dozens of times each second. This bird has a maximum heart rate of 1000 beats per minute.

Sugar-water feeders and tube-shaped flowers can attract hummingbirds to your backyard. Hummingbirds poke their long, thin bills into flowers and drink nectar using their tongues.

Females have a shiny green back and light-colored belly. Only the males have a bright red throat.

These birds make their nests out of lichens and spiderwebs. The spiderwebs allow the nest to stretch as the babies grow!

Q: Why do hummingbirds hum?
A: Because they can't remember the words!

21

Downy Woodpecker

Downy and Hairy woodpeckers look very similar. Size is the best way to tell them apart. The Downy Woodpecker is smaller and more likely a backyard visitor.

Male Downy Woodpeckers have a red patch at the back of the head. Males spend their time on the smaller branches, and females spend more time on tree trunks and larger branches.

A pair of Downy Woodpeckers will carve out their nest hole in soft, rotting wood. Dead or dying trees are important places for many birds and animals to find shelter.

The Downy Woodpecker's favorite backyard food is suet, but it will also eat peanuts, millet and black oil sunflower seeds. These are just treats, though. Insects make up most of its diet.

23

Northern Flicker

The Northern Flicker's favorite food is ants, so it spends a lot of time on the ground. It will also eat suet, sunflower seeds or peanuts at bird feeders.

Like most woodpeckers, the Northern Flicker has a really long tongue. The tongue is coated with sticky saliva that helps it catch the insects it likes to eat.

The Northern Flicker usually carves out its own nest in a tree, but it can also be attracted to a backyard nest box.

Nestlings are fed ant larvae that the parent carries in its crop.

Pileated Woodpecker

The **Pileated Woodpecker** has a red crest and is the size of a crow. This impressive bird is the sixth-largest woodpecker in the world.

These birds make large, oval-shaped nest holes.

Pileated Woodpeckers feed on carpenter ants. Trees where they feed sometimes have huge, rectangular holes that can be as long as a baseball bat as in this photo!

Other species, like Wood Ducks, American Kestrels and even flying squirrels will nest in abandoned Pileated Woodpecker holes.

27

Great Crested Flycatcher

The **Great Crested Flycatcher's** **loud, rising** wheep. **is easy to hear, but this bird is hard to spot. Look way, way up! This large flycatcher spends most of its time high in the forest canopy.**

This bird usually nests in tree cavities but will also use nest boxes. Sometimes it decorates the nest entrance with snakeskin or plastic wrap!

Watch for this bird swooping out from tree branches to catch flying insects. It also eats small fruit, then vomits up the pits. Yuk!

Red-eyed Vireo

The Red-eyed Vireo's eye doesn't turn red until it is about 9 or 10 months old.

The Red-eyed Vireo eats mostly insects in the summer. In the winter, it flies to South America and switches to a diet of mostly fruit.

The male Red-eyed Vireo can out-sing any of his neighbors and can sing 40 phrases every minute. One male was recorded singing over 20,000 songs in one day!

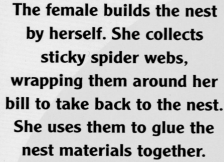

The female builds the nest by herself. She collects sticky spider webs, wrapping them around her bill to take back to the nest. She uses them to glue the nest materials together.

Blue Jay

The beautiful, noisy Blue Jay is a well-known visitor to backyards. Jays can be very bossy, chasing smaller birds or squirrels away from feeders. Mobs of jays will even pester Great-horned Owls!

When nesting, the Blue Jay becomes quiet and secretive. Its eggs are bluish or greenish with darker markings.

Jays cache nuts to save for winter snacking. This activity is important to the forest ecosystem. In the fall, one jay may bury thousands of acorns, then forget where most are hidden. These acorns will then grow into oak trees!

33

American Crow

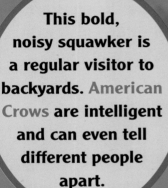

This bold, noisy squawker is a regular visitor to backyards. American Crows are intelligent and can even tell different people apart.

Crows are best known for making a caw sound, but these clever birds can mimic many sounds. They can whine like a dog and laugh or cry like a human!

You may see this bird stealing pet food from a dog dish or taking peanuts or fruit left out for other birds. Given a chance, they will fly off with your lunch or rip open a garbage bag to eat the food scraps inside.

Q: Why did the crow stand on the telephone pole? A: He wanted to make a long-distance caw.

35

Barn Swallow

The Barn Swallow eats mostly insects that it catches while flying. It is fond of eggshells, too. If you crush eggshells and place them outside, this swallow may come take them.

In flight, you can tell the Barn Swallow from other swallows because its tail is forked. Its outside feathers are much longer than the inside feathers.

Barn Swallows once nested in caves. Now they often nest on buildings or under bridges. They make their nests by rolling mud into small balls and sticking them together one mouthful at a time.

Chicks leave the nest at about 3 weeks old. By about a month old, the young can catch their own food.

37

Black-capped Chickadee

The Black-capped Chickadee is a common backyard bird. It is easily attracted to feeders for sunflower seeds, suet and peanuts.

When you hear this bird's chick-a-dee-dee call, you will know where its name comes from! If you hear more dee notes at the end, it means the bird is trying to warn its flock mates of danger.

The female uses moss and fur to line her nest. Both parents catch insects to feed their young. The parents keep feeding their young for up to a month after they leave the nest.

The Black-capped Chickadee hides food for the cold winter months. It has a great memory and can remember where all its food is hidden!

Tufted Titmouse

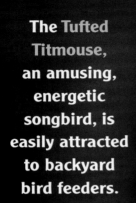

The **Tufted Titmouse,** an amusing, energetic songbird, is easily attracted to backyard bird feeders.

Titmice pairs stay together all year. Young may stay with their parents for more than a year, helping to raise newborn chicks.

This bird nests in cavities and will also use nest boxes. If you want to build your own birdhouse, search the Internet to find plans and learn how to make a safe nesting box.

Titmice are common in the deciduous forests of the eastern United States. They are expanding their range north into southern Canada, where they are seen in oak forests and at feeders.

41

Red-breasted Nuthatch

The Red-breasted Nuthatch eats mostly insects in the summer and seeds in the fall and winter. It will happily take seeds, suet and peanuts from feeders year-round.

This bird makes a nasal yank yank sound. A breeding pair stays together all year long, and they often talk to each other.

The Red-breasted Nuthatch carves out its own nest cavity and smears the nest entrance with sticky tree resin. It sometimes steals nest-lining material from the nests of other birds!

White-breasted Nuthatch

Nuthatches are nicknamed upside-down birds **because they often go down the trunks of trees headfirst.** White-breasted Nuthatches **do not have the black eye band of the Red-breasted Nuthatch.**

Nuthatches will hammer a nut with their bills to hatch the nut open. That's how they earned the name nuthatch.

This bird stores food for the winter. It hides the food, often seeds or nuts, in bark crevices or other good hiding places. It will also cover the food with moss, lichen or a sliver of bark.

45

House Wren

The House Wren is a common backyard visitor. It searches for spiders and caterpillars in gardens and bushes.

This bird is a plain, brown bird with a beautiful, bubbly song. It usually holds its tail up when perched or standing.

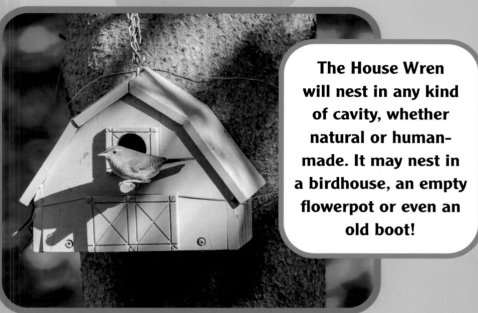

The House Wren will nest in any kind of cavity, whether natural or human-made. It may nest in a birdhouse, an empty flowerpot or even an old boot!

This bird lines its nest with feathers, grass and hair. Sometimes spider egg sacs are added to the nest as well!

47

Golden-crowned Kinglet

The Golden-crowned Kinglet is tiny, barely larger than a hummingbird! It is named for its yellow crown.

Q: Why do boy birds look like their dad?
A: Like feather, like son!

These hardy birds nest in the boreal forest and spend the winter in the woodlands of North America. They can lower their body temperature at night to conserve energy!

Kinglets are always moving. You can identify them by their constant motion and nervous wing flicking.

49

Eastern Bluebird

The lovely Eastern Bluebird sings a soft, pleasing warble. The male has a deep blue back and a warm, reddish breast. Females are duller, and young birds have spots on their breasts.

Bluebirds were once common. There are fewer bluebirds now because of habitat loss and competition with House Sparrows and European Starlings for natural nest cavities.

Look for nest boxes attached to fence posts and utility poles along rural roads. Bluebird nest boxes are easy to make and are helping to boost populations of this cavity-nesting bird.

Watch for bluebirds perched on wires or fence posts. Bluebirds eat mainly insects, catching them in midair or fluttering to the ground.

51

American Robin

An **American Robin** may come to your bird feeder, but you are more likely to see it pulling earthworms out of your lawn, especially after it rains.

Both the female and male have red bellies and gray upperparts, but the female is paler overall. The robin's song sounds a bit like cheerily, cheer up, cheer up, cheerily, cheer up!

The female builds the nest and lays 3 to 5 eggs. Both parents feed the chicks. Nestlings beg for food by stretching their necks up high and opening their mouths wide.

Young robins leave the nest at about 2 weeks old. The parents continue to feed them for another 3 weeks or more.

Gray Catbird

The Gray Catbird doesn't often visit feeders, but it will take fruit or mealworms if they are offered. This gray bird has a black cap and a cinnamon brown patch under its tail.

This bird makes a mew call that sounds a lot like a cat. Its song can include imitations of other birds as well as mechanical sounds. And it can sing with 2 voices at once!

The Gray Catbird comes to eastern North America in the spring and summer to nest. Young catbirds leave the nest at about 10 days old. Chicks are fed insects and spiders.

55

European Starling

In the fall, the European Starling grows new feathers that have whitish tips. By the time spring rolls around, the white tips have worn off, leaving only the glossy black part of the feathers.

The European Starling was brought to North America about 130 years ago. It is a common visitor to backyard feeders and isn't fussy about food.

European Starlings like to gather in groups and are good imitators. They often imitate the songs of other bird species. Like parrots, they can even mimic human speech.

European Starlings are cavity nesters. They nest in tree cavities and holes in buildings or cliffs.

57

Cedar Waxwing

Most birds will remove seeds from
fruits, but not the Cedar Waxwing. It
just swallows them and poops them out.

Not all birds need to drink water, but the Cedar Waxwing needs to drink water or eat snow to balance out the high sugar content of the fruit it eats. It also really likes to take baths!

Cedar Waxwings nest in loose groups of 12 or more birds. To save time, females will sometimes steal nesting material from the nests of other bird species.

Yellow-rumped Warbler

The male Yellow-rumped Warbler is darker overall than the female, with a black mask and a white throat. Both males and females have yellow patches on their rumps and sides.

The female is lighter gray-brown overall, with less dark streaking on her chest.

This bird spends time in forests or near water. In the summer, it breeds across Canada and the northeastern United States. It flies south for the winter.

The Yellow-rumped Warbler may come to your yard for a bath. If you have a birdbath, it is important to change the water every few days to keep it clean.

Common Yellowthroat

The Common Yellowthroat is a vocal bird. It belts out a distinct witchety-witchety-witchety song while perched on top of a tall cattail or shrub.

This tiny bird has bright yellow underparts and an olive green back. The male's distinctive black mask makes him look like a bandit!

In the summer, this bird lurks around marshes and hides in tangled vegetation.

You can coax these curious birds out of hiding by making a squeak or pishhh sound.

Eastern Towhee

Eastern Towhees are colorful sparrows that prefer to feed on the ground. They hop along in the leaf litter, searching for food. Listen for this noisy bird rustling around in the undergrowth.

Towhees prefer overgrown backyards with bushy borders or shrubs. They usually build their nests on the ground.

The male is more richly colored than the female. Juveniles are brownish gray with pale orange markings. Most Eastern Towhees have red eyes, but some that live in Georgia and Florida have yellow eyes.

The Eastern Towhee eats all kinds of food, like wiggly centipedes and slimy snails. They also eat flower buds, seeds, fruit, acorns or grain.

65

Chipping Sparrow

You can tell the Chipping Sparrow apart from other sparrows that visit your yard by its reddish brown cap. It regularly eats seeds from feeders or on the ground.

The Chipping Sparrow eats mostly insects in the summer while raising its young.

Both parents feed the nestlings seeds and insects. Young leave the nest when they are about 10 days old.

The Chipping Sparrow is named for its chip contact call. It uses this call to stay in contact with family and flock mates.

Song Sparrow

Song sparrows are one of our most common and adaptable sparrows. To identify this bird, look for a bold, central breast spot and streaks down its chest.

Song sparrows are named for their bright sweet, sweet, sweet songs. Young males learn to sing by listening to their fathers or other males, then they develop their own tunes.

Song Sparrows that live in wet, coastal climates have darker plumage. Darker feathers contain a pigment called melanin that makes the feathers tougher and resistant to wear.

White-throated Sparrow

White-throated Sparrows **often visit backyard bird feeders. Look for these birds on the ground, scratching for fallen sunflower seeds, insects or spiders. They even eat snails!**

This bird breeds across Canada and spends the winter in the eastern United States. During breeding season, the male whistles a distinct Oh sweet Canada Canada **song.**

This bird comes in two color forms. One has black and white stripes on the head. The other has brown and tan stripes.

Q: What do you give a sick bird?
A: Tweetment!

71

Dark-eyed Junco

The Dark-eyed Junco is a common visitor to backyards and bird feeders, especially in the winter. It eats a variety of seeds, nuts and grains.

The Dark-eyed Junco comes in different color forms. The form common in the east is mostly grey with a white belly.

The female usually builds her nest on the ground. Some nests are well built, but others are flimsy. She lays 3 to 6 brown-spotted eggs in her nest.

After she incubates the eggs for about 12 days, the nestlings hatch. Both parents feed nestlings predigested food or insects.

Scarlet Tanager

Tanagers are stunning birds. The male Scarlet Tanager is a brilliant red, with shiny black wings and a black tail. The flashy male gets his red color from the food he eats!

This bird eats mainly ants, butterflies, moths, cicadas, dragonflies, earthworms and some fruit.

The female is a dull olive color with dark wings and tail. The female builds a nest out of twigs and grasses in the crook of a tree.

Like other birds, tanagers enjoy taking baths. If you have a bird bath, you might get lucky and see one of these scarlet visitors!

Northern Cardinal

The Northern Cardinal is one of the most widely recognized birds. Males are a brilliant red, and females and young are brown with a reddish tinge.

The male raises his crest and sings softly to attract a mate. He may offer the female a seed to show that he can provide for the young!

Northern Cardinals form close pair bonds. Some couples stay together year-round, singing to each other with soft whistles.

The female builds her nest with twigs carried in by the male. After she incubates the eggs, the male feeds and cares for the young.

77

Rose-breasted Grosbeak

The Rose-breasted Grosbeak sounds like a robin that has taken singing lessons! Listen for grosbeaks to find them. They spend most of their time high in the leafy canopy.

Males are black and white, with a bold, reddish-pink V-shaped patch on their breast.

Q: Why do birds fly south for the winter?
A: Because it's too far to walk!

Females are brown and streaked. Both males and females have a large, cone-shaped bill.

These birds can be seen in eastern North America in the summer and during migration. Watch for them in forests, parks, orchards and at feeders. In the winter, grosbeaks fly south to Mexico and South America.

Red-winged Blackbird

The male Red-winged Blackbird is easy to recognize with his bright red-and-yellow wing patch and his loud conk-la-ree call.

The female is brown and buff with a pale eyebrow.

The Red-winged Blackbird eats mostly insects in the summer and mostly plant food—seeds or grains—in the winter.

When they hatch, nestlings cannot see and have very little down to keep them warm. Two weeks after hatching, when they leave the nest, they can see well and have a full set of flight feathers.

Common Grackle

Common Grackles are large blackbirds that have shiny, iridescent feathers that gleam in the sun. Males have bluish heads and bronze bodies. Females are similar but less iridescent.

Grackles are common in North America, especially in cities, towns and farmlands. They prefer forested areas near ponds, marshes or creeks.

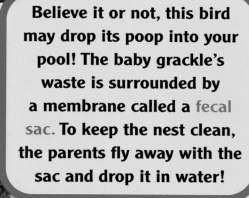

Believe it or not, this bird may drop its poop into your pool! The baby grackle's waste is surrounded by a membrane called a fecal sac. To keep the nest clean, the parents fly away with the sac and drop it in water!

Brown-headed Cowbird

The male Brown-headed Cowbird has a brown head and a black body. The female is pale brown all over. This bird eats seeds, grain or peanuts from backyard bird feeders.

This bird earned the name cowbird and the nickname Buffalo Bird because it likes to be near livestock. It eats the insects that these animals flush up as they move through the tall grass.

The Brown-headed Cowbird female lays her eggs in the nests of other birds and lets those parents raise her chicks. She can lay up to 40 eggs per season in many, many nests!

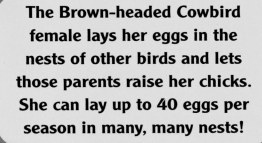

Brown-headed Cowbird chicks hatch early and grow quickly. They often grow to be larger than their adoptive parents!

**85**

Baltimore Oriole

This bird builds a hanging nest, shaped like a pouch. The female weaves together hundreds of fibers, making a delicate cradle for her young.

Baltimore Orioles feed their babies fruit and all kinds of insects, like beetles, moths and even wasps! Insects are high in proteins that the baby birds need to grow.

In spring and fall, orioles eat more fruit and nectar. Their body turns these sugary foods into fats and stores them. These fat reserves supply fuel for the bird's migration south to Mexico or South America!

This bird has a clear, flute-like whistle. Listen for them where there are large trees, even in city parks.

House Finch

The male House Finch's plumage can vary from bright red to yellowish. Females are brown and streaky. The bright colors come from carotenoids—yellow, orange or red pigments—in the food it eats.

Q: How do birds pay at a restaurant? A: With their bills!

Many birds sing
during the
spring breeding
season to mark their
territory and attract
a mate, but the male
House Finch sings
his cheerful song all
year-round.

This bird thrives in urban places. The
pair builds a messy nest among house
eaves, rafters or chimneys.

89

Common Redpoll

Common Redpolls are most often seen in winter, but they are unpredictable. Some years, large flocks of these birds appear, and other years there are only a few.

Watch for groups of redpolls at backyard feeders or in bushes, searching for food. These tiny birds have very little body fat. They must eat constantly in winter to stay warm.

In bitterly cold weather, redpolls fluff out their feathers to trap layers of warm air near their skin.

Q: What's a bird's favorite game?
A: Beak-a-boo!

American Goldfinch

The **American Goldfinch** is a seed eater that often visits bird feeders. It will also perch on sunflowers or thistles to eat the fresh seeds.

In the summer, the male is bright yellow with a black cap. The female is an olive green color. Both have black wings and tail.

The call of the American Goldfinch sounds like po-ta-to-chip. In the spring, the male sings a song of twitters and warbles to attract a mate.

In the winter, the American Goldfinch male has much drabber, grayer plumage.

House Sparrow

House Sparrows were brought to North America from Europe more than 150 years ago. Now they are common in cities and towns across the U.S. and Canada. These birds often visit backyard feeders.

The male House Sparrow has a black throat and bib. The female is brown and beige overall.

House Sparrows often look for food in groups. Males with larger black bib patches are older and have a higher rank within the group.

The House Sparrow mostly nests in holes in buildings, but it will sometimes use nest boxes or traffic lights.

The Publisher: KidsWorld Books

Library and Archives Canada Cataloguing in Publication
Title: Backyard birds of the East / Krista Einstein & Genevieve Einstein.
Names: Einstein, Krista, 1972– author. | Einstein, Genevieve, 1977– author.
Identifiers: Canadiana 20210323663 | ISBN 9781988183633 (softcover)
Subjects: LCSH: Birds—Canada, Eastern—Identification—Juvenile literature. | LCSH: Birds—East (U.S.)—Identification—Juvenile literature. | LCSH: Birds—Canada, Eastern—Juvenile literature. | LCSH: Birds—East (U.S.)—Juvenile literature. | LCGFT: Field guides.
Classification: LCC QL685.W47 E46 2021 | DDC j598.09713—dc23

Image credits
Front cover: GettyImages: BrianEKushner. *Back cover:* GettyImages: BrianLasenby, Eric Santin, Christiane Godin.
Bird Illustrations: Gary Ross, Ted Nordhagen, Ewa Pluciennik, Horst Krause
Photo Credits: From GettyImages: Peter Milota, Jr 8, Motionshooter-juvenile 9b, passion4nature 10b, SC Shank 10a, Devonyu 11, Tempau 12b, Christiane Godin 12a, Janet Griffin-Scott 16b, zhuclear 17a, Janet Griffin-Scott 17b, iculizard 18a, Karen Hogan 18b, Dennis Stogsdill 19b, summersetretrievers 19a, MattCuda 20b, CarolinaBirdman 20a, ehrlif 21b, Luc Pouliot 21a, blightylad-infocus 22a, Thomas Anderson 22b, R Lolli Morrow 23a, Ken Griffiths 24b, Alberthep 25, Harry Collins 26b, Christiane Godin 26a, petrovval 27a, Harry Collins 27b, 6381380 28, Karel Bock 29b, passion4nature 29a, creighton359 30a, OldFulica 31b, BrianEKushner 32, Karen Hogan 33b, David Tran 33a, William Krumpelman 36a, drakuliren 36b, Edward Palm 37a, Heather Burditt 37b, Rebecca Turner 38a, JeffGoulden 38b, ChrisBoswell 39a, JenDeVos 39b, erniedecker 40a, SteveByland 41b, PaulReevesPhotography 42a, Devonyu 42b, RLSPHOTO 44, BrianLasenby 46a, Jeff Edwards 46b, Ralph Navarro 47a, Carol Hamilton 47b, PaulReevesPhotography 48, Devonyu 49b, RalfWeigel 49a, SteveByland 50a, MelodyanneM 50b, BrianLasenby 51a, SteveByland 51b, spates 52b, Mason Maron 52a, mtruchon 53a, Warren_Price 53b, BrianLasenby 54b, SteveByland 54a, Heather Burditt 55, BrianEKushner 56a, EJ_Rodriquez 56b, bazilfoto 57a, Thorsten Spoerlein 57b, LorraineHudgins 58, Warren_Price 59a, Silfox 60, lrh847 60, Jean Landry 62b, johnandersonphoto 62a, MichaelStubblefield 64a, SteveByland 65a, BrianLasenby 65b, mirceax 67b, PaulReevesPhotography 70a, Trevor_Jones_ Photo 70b, BrianEKushner 71, Irving A Gaffney 72b, BrianEKushner 72a, BethWolff43 73b, yhelfman 73a, BrianLasenby 74, MichaelStubblefield 75b, J Esteban Berrio 75a, SteveByland 76a, Jupiterimages 77b, SteveByland 77a, BrianLasenby 78, BrianLasenby 79a, Hurricane 79b, DavidByronKeener 80b, ca2hill 80a, passion4nature 81, Christopher R Mazza 83a, ebettini 84b, PamSchodt 85b, danlogan 86a, LillianCTaylor 86b, McKinneMike 87a, CathyKeifer 88, Dee Carpenter Photography 90a, Chiyacat 92b, Edward Palm 92a, RCKeller 93a, davidhaas383 93b, Sloot 94a, PaulFleet 94b, shellhawker 95a, Oren Ravid 95b. From Flickr: Mike's Birds 9a, CheepShot 13b, USFWS Mountain-Prairie 13a, Allan Hack 14, David Slater 15a, John Liu 15b, Courtney Celley USFWS 16a, Courtney Celley USFWS 23b, Shawn McCready 24a, Laura Wolf 30b, Felix Uribe 31a, cuatrok77 34b, Becky Matsubara 34a, cuatrok77 35, Under the same moon 40b, Kelly Verdeck 41a, David A Mitchell 43, David A Mitchell 45b, Yanech Gary 45a, FancyLady 59b, U.S. Fish and Wildlife Service Northeast Region 61, Tracie Hall 61, Becky Matsubara 63b, California Department of Fish and Wildlife 63a, USFWS Midwest Region 64b, F D Richards 66b, malibuskiboats 66a, Dennis Murphy 67a, Kelly Colgan Azar 68b, Veit 68a, 611catbirds, too 69, Nigel 76b, Shenandoah National Park 82, Gary Leavens 83b, nature80020 84a, Krista Lundgren USFWS 85a, Scott Heron 87b, Veit 89a, mma Forsberg 90b, Andy Reago & Chrissy McClarren 91. From Wikimedia Commons: Kelly Teague 89b.

Icons: GettyImages: Alexander_Kizilov; ChoochartSansong, rashadashurov, MerggyR, agrino, lioputra, FORGEM, Stevy, Intpro, MaksimYremenko, Oceloti, Thomas Lydell, Sudowoodo.

We acknowledge the financial support of the Government of Canada.
Nous reconnaissons l'appui financier du gouvernement du Canada.

Funded by the Government of Canada
Financé par le gouvernement du Canada | Canadä

Printed in China

PC: 38-1